First World War
and Army of Occupation
War Diary
France, Belgium and Germany

57 DIVISION
170 Infantry Brigade
Loyal North Lancashire Regiment
4/5th Battalion (Territorial Force)
22 October 1915 - 29 February 1916

WO95/2979/4

The Naval & Military Press Ltd
www.nmarchive.com
Published in association with The National Archives

Published by

The Naval & Military Press Ltd

Unit 10 Ridgewood Industrial Park,

Uckfield, East Sussex,

TN22 5QE England

Tel: +44 (0) 1825 749494

www.naval-military-press.com

www.nmarchive.com

This diary has been reprinted in facsimile from the original. Any imperfections are inevitably reproduced and the quality may fall short of modern type and cartographic standards.

© **Crown Copyright**
Images reproduced by permission of The National Archives, London, England, 2015.

Contents

Document type	Place/Title	Date From	Date To
Heading	WO95/2979/4		
Heading	War Diary Of 4/5 Battalion Loyal North Lancashire Regt. From 22nd October 1915 To 31st October 1915 Volume I		
War Diary	Ashford	22/10/1915	22/10/1915
War Diary	Ashford Victoria Park	25/10/1915	27/10/1915
War Diary	Ashford	31/10/1915	31/10/1915
Heading	War Diary Of 4/5 Battalion Loyal North Lancashire Regiment From 1st November 1915 To 30th November 1915 (Volume I)		
War Diary	Ashford	01/11/1915	30/11/1915
Heading	War Diary Of 4/5 Battalion Loyal North Lancashire Regt. From 1st December-31st December 1915 (Volume I)		
War Diary	Ashford	01/12/1915	31/12/1915
Heading	War Diary Of 4/5 Battalion Loyal North Lancashire Regiment From 1st January 1916 To 31st January 1916 Volume 2		
War Diary	Ashford	01/01/1916	31/01/1916
Heading	War Diary Of 4/5 Battalion Loyal North Lancashire Regt. From 1st February 1916 To 29th February 1916 (Volume 2)		
War Diary	Ashford	01/02/1916	29/02/1916

WD 95/29779(4)

WD 95/29779(4)

No UDE

Confidential

War Diary
of
4/5 Battalion Loyal North Lancashire Regt.
from 22nd October 1915 to 31st October 1915.

Volume I

Army Form C. 2118.

WAR DIARY
or
INTELLIGENCE SUMMARY
(Erase heading not required.)

Instructions regarding War Diaries and Intelligence Summaries are contained in F. S. Regs., Part II. and the Staff Manual respectively. Title pages will be prepared in manuscript.

Hour, Date, Place	Summary of Events and Information	Remarks and references to Appendices
Arrived ASHFORD 4.30. am. 22 October. 1915	The Battalion (22 Officers 875 Other Ranks) left BOLTON in two trains on the night of 21st October 1915. A transport Section of 1 Officer & 28 men preceded the Battalion, also an advance Party of 2 Officers & 30 men.	Col: J. Wybergh 9/Loyls: Col: H. Wybergh 9/Loyls:
ASHFORD. 11. am. 25 October 1915. VICTORIA PARK	The Brigadier made his "Marching in" inspection.	
ASHFORD. 10. am 26 October 1915. VICTORIA PARK	The Brigadier inspected A & B. coys: in Marching Order. I saw their kits.	Col: H. Wybergh 9/Loyls:
ASHFORD. 10. am 27 October 1915. VICTORIA PARK	The Brigadier inspected C & D coys: in Marching Order. I saw their kits	Col: H. Wybergh 9/Loyls:
ASHFORD. 31. Oct 15.		

J. Wybergh
Lieut: Colonel,
Comdg: 4/5th Loyal North Lanc. Regt.

Confidential

War Diary
of.
4/5 Battalion Loyal North Lancashire Regiment
from 1st November 1915 to 30th November 1915.

(Volume I)

Army Form C. 2118.

WAR DIARY
or
INTELLIGENCE SUMMARY

(Erase heading not required.)

Instructions regarding War Diaries and Intelligence Summaries are contained in F. S. Regs., Part II. and the Staff Manual respectively. Title pages will be prepared in manuscript.

Hour, Date, Place	Summary of Events and Information	Remarks and references to Appendices
1915.		
1st Nov. Ashford.		Lt.Col.
2nd Nov. Ashford.	Nil	Lt.Col.
3rd Nov. Ashford.	Nil	Lt.Col.
4th Nov. Ashford.	Nil	Lt.Col.
5th Nov. Ashford.	Nil	Lt.Col.
6th Nov. Ashford.	Nil	Lt.Col.
7th Nov. Ashford.	Nil	Lt.Col.
8th Nov. Ashford.	Nil	Lt.Col.
9th Nov. Ashford.	Nil	Lt.Col.
10th Nov. Ashford.	Nil	Lt.Col.
11th Nov. Ashford.	Nil	Lt.Col.
12th Nov. Ashford.	Nil	Lt.Col.
13th Nov. Ashford.	Nil	Lt.Col.
14th Nov. Ashford.	Nil	Lt.Col.
15th Nov. Ashford.	Nil	Lt.Col.

Army Form C. 2118.

WAR DIARY
or
INTELLIGENCE SUMMARY

(Erase heading not required.)

Instructions regarding War Diaries and Intelligence Summaries are contained in F. S. Regs., Part II. and the Staff Manual respectively. Title pages will be prepared in manuscript.

Hour, Date, Place	Summary of Events and Information	Remarks and references to Appendices
10 am. 16th Nov. Ashford	Received Orders for hand in all Japanese (256) rifles at once. As 303 rifles might be expected at any moment. This was carried out.	N/A
17. Nov. Ashford	Nil	N/A
19. Nov. Ashford	As the 303 Rifles had not arrived, the Japanese (256) rifles were re-distributed.	N/A
9.30 pm ditto ditto	Received Orders for all Japanese Rifles & Ammunition to be packed up ready & despatched to Weedon. Men worked all night.	N/A
7 am 20th Nov. Ashford	The above work was completed, & the Rifles & Ammunition despatched at 9 am.	N/A
21st Nov. Ashford	Nil.	N/A
3.15 pm 22nd Nov. Ashford	The Inspector General of Infantry (Major General L. J. Dickson) Inspected the Battalion at Watch Park and on Parade & at Drill & congratulated the Officer Commanding on their Steadiness & smart appearance, considering the short time the Battalion had been in existence.	N/A

Army Form C. 2118.

WAR DIARY
or
INTELLIGENCE SUMMARY
(Erase heading not required.)

Instructions regarding War Diaries and Intelligence Summaries are contained in F. S. Regs., Part II. and the Staff Manual respectively. Title pages will be prepared in manuscript.

Hour, Date, Place	Summary of Events and Information	Remarks and references to Appendices
23. Nov. Ashford.	Nil	Nil M.
24. Nov. Ashford.	Nil	Nil M.
25. Nov. Ashford.	Nil	Nil M.
26. Nov. Ashford.	Nil	Nil M.
27. Nov. Ashford.	Nil	Nil M.
28. Nov. Ashford.	Nil	Nil M.
29. Nov. Ashford.	Nil	Nil M.
30. Nov. Ashford.	Nil	Nil M.

Ashford.
30. Nov. 15.

C H Long Evans
Lieut Colonel,
Comdg 4/5th Loyal North Lancs Regt.

Confidential

War Diary
of
4/5 Battalion Loyal North Lancashire Regt.
from 1st December – 31st December.
1915
(Volume I)

Army Form C. 2118.

WAR DIARY
or
INTELLIGENCE SUMMARY

(Erase heading not required.)

Instructions regarding War Diaries and Intelligence Summaries are contained in F. S. Regs., Part II. and the Staff Manual respectively. Title pages will be prepared in manuscript.

Hour, Date, Place	Summary of Events and Information	Remarks and references to Appendices
1st Dec ASHFORD.	nil	Lieut. Col. Myers O.C. Sqdn.
2nd December ASHFORD	nil	Lieut. Col. Myers O.C. Sqdn.
3rd December ASHFORD	Inspection of Battalion Books by O.C. 57th West Lancashire Division, who expressed himself as quite satisfied.	
ditto	12 Officers left this dg. for Blackpool to join the 3rd Line (3/5 Sept North Lancashire Regt) on reduction of Establishment	Lieut. Col. Myers O.C. Sqdn.
4th December ASHFORD	nil	Lieut. Col. Myers O.C. Sqdn.
5th December ASHFORD	nil	Lieut. Col. Myers O.C. Sqdn.
6th December ASHFORD	nil	Lieut. Col. Myers O.C. Sqdn.
7th December ASHFORD	Observation Post at PEASMARSH near RYE (1 Officer & men) relieved by 1st Devon Yeomanry	Lieut. Col. Myers O.C. Sqdn.
8th December ASHFORD	nil	Lieut. Col. Myers O.C. Sqdn.
9th December ASHFORD	nil	Lieut. Col. Myers O.C. Sqdn.
10th December ASHFORD	nil	Lieut. Col. Myers O.C. Sqdn.
11th December ASHFORD	nil	Lieut. Col. Myers O.C. Sqdn.
12th December ASHFORD	nil	Lieut. Col. Myers O.C. Sqdn.

Army Form C. 2118.

WAR DIARY
or
INTELLIGENCE SUMMARY
(Erase heading not required.)

Instructions regarding War Diaries and Intelligence Summaries are contained in F. S. Regs.; Part II. and the Staff Manual respectively. Title pages will be prepared in manuscript.

Hour, Date, Place	Summary of Events and Information	Remarks and references to Appendices
9.30 a.m. 13 December ASHFORD	200 N.C.O's & men proceeded to BLACKPOOL to join the 3rd line (3/5 Loyal North Lancashire Regt) on reduction of establishment.	W.H. Meyer O/Capt
14 December ASHFORD	3 O.C. 5.7= (West Lancashire) Division inspected a company at Drill	W.H. Meyer O/Capt
15 December ASHFORD	nil	W.H. Meyer O/Capt
16 December ASHFORD	nil	W.H. Meyer O/Capt
17 December ASHFORD	nil	W.H. Meyer O/Capt
18 December ASHFORD	nil	W.H. Meyer O/Capt
19 December ASHFORD	nil	W.H. Meyer O/Capt
9.40 p.m. 20 December ASHFORD	Brigade night alarm - Bttn to March off at 11.30 p.m.	W.H. Meyer O/Capt
21 December ASHFORD	nil	W.H. Meyer O/Capt
22 December ASHFORD	nil	W.H. Meyer O/Capt
23rd December ASHFORD	nil	W.H. Meyer O/Capt
24= December ASHFORD	nil	W.H. Meyer O/Capt
25= December ASHFORD	nil	W.H. Meyer O/Capt
26= December ASHFORD	nil	W.H. Meyer O/Capt
27= December ASHFORD	nil	W.H. Meyer O/Capt
28= December ASHFORD	nil	W.H. Meyer O/Capt
29= December ASHFORD	nil	W.H. Meyer O/Capt
30= December ASHFORD	nil	6W.H. Meyer O/Capt
31st December ASHFORD	nil	W.H. Meyer O/Capt

Lieut: **Colonel**,
Comdg **4/5th Loyal North Lanc. Regt.**

Confidential

War Diary
of

4/5 Battalion Royal North Lancashire Regiment

from 1st January 1916 to 31st January 1916.

Volume 2.

C46

Army Form C. 2118

WAR DIARY
or
INTELLIGENCE SUMMARY

(Erase heading not required.)

Instructions regarding War Diaries and Intelligence Summaries are contained in F. S. Regs., Part II. and the Staff Manual respectively. Title Pages will be prepared in manuscript.

Place	Date 1916.	Hour	Summary of Events and Information	Remarks and references to Appendices
ASHFORD	1 Jan	—	NIL.	Col.A.
"	2 Jan	—	NIL.	Col.A.
"	3 Jan	—	Nil.	Col.A.
"	4 Jan	—	NIL.	Col.A.
"	5 Jan	—	NIL	Col.A.
"	6 Jan	—	NIL	Col.A.
"	7 Jan	—	NIL	Col.A.
"	8 Jan	—	NIL.	Col.A.
"	9 Jan	—	NIL.	Col.A.
"	10 Jan	—	NIL.	Col.A.
"	11 Jan	—	NIL	Col.A.
"	12 Jan	—	NIL	Col.A.
"	13 Jan	1.30pm	Inspection by B.G.C. 2nd Army at HATCH PARK - ASHFORD - The G.O.C expressed himself as satisfied with his inspection of the Battalion.	Col.A.
"	14 Jan	—	NIL.	Col.A.

1875 Wt. W593/826 1,000,000 4/15 J.B.C. & A. A.D.S.S./Forms/C. 2118.

Army Form C. 2118

WAR DIARY
or
INTELLIGENCE SUMMARY
(Erase heading not required.)

Instructions regarding War Diaries and Intelligence Summaries are contained in F. S. Regs., Part II. and the Staff Manual respectively. Title Pages will be prepared in manuscript.

Place	Date 1916	Hour	Summary of Events and Information	Remarks and references to Appendices
ASHFORD	15 Jan	11.55 pm	Zeppelins reported in the vicinity of DOVER. Usual precautions taken	Nil
"	16 Jan	—	nil	Nil
"	17 Jan	—	nil	Nil
"	18 Jan	—	nil	Nil
"	19 Jan	—	nil	Nil
"	20 Jan	—	nil	Nil
"	21 Jan	—	nil	Nil
"	22 Jan	—	nil	Nil
"	23 Jan	2.I pm	Zeppelins reported in the vicinity of DOVER. Usual precautions taken - fire alarm - Brigade fire alarm sent. Necessary tools at 3.40 pm	Nil
"	24 Jan	5.30 pm	nil	Nil
"	25 Jan	—	nil	Nil
"	26 Jan	—	nil	Nil
"	27 Jan	—	nil	Nil
"	28 Jan	9.5 pm	Zeppelins reported proceeding S.W. from SHEERNESS - All lights extinguished by order of Police - Usual precautions taken	Nil
"	29 Jan	—	nil	Nil
"	30 Jan	—	Nil	Nil
"	31 Jan	10 am	Battalion inspected by B.S.G. 170 Infantry Brigade in GODINGTON PARK. 28 DERBY recruits arrived from BOLTON	Nil

Colly d. Marford
Major
Comdg. 4/5th Loyal North Lanc. Regt.

Lieut-Colonel,

Confidential

War Diary
of.
4/5 Battalion Loyal North Lancashire Regt:
from 1st February 1916 to 29th February 1916.

(Volume 2.)

Army Form C. 2118

WAR DIARY
or
INTELLIGENCE SUMMARY

(Erase heading not required.)

Instructions regarding War Diaries and Intelligence Summaries are contained in F.S. Regs., Part II. and the Staff Manual respectively. Title Pages will be prepared in manuscript.

Place	Date	Hour	Summary of Events and Information	Remarks and references to Appendices
ASHFORD	1.2.16		Nil	Cell.Mgr Bayf
ASHFORD	2.2.16	9 am	2nd Batch of Derby Recruits arrived from BOLTON (number 12)	Cell.M.
ASHFORD	3.2.16		Nil	Cell.M.
ASHFORD	4.2.16		Nil	Cell.M.
ASHFORD	5.2.16	9 am	3rd Batch of Derby Recruits arrived from BOLTON (number 27)	Cell.M.
ASHFORD	6.2.16		Nil	Cell.M.
ASHFORD	7.2.16	12.25am	Observation post discontinued at ASHFORD & moved to MARDEN	Cell.M.
ASHFORD	8.2.16	9 am	4th Batch of Derby Recruits arrived from BOLTON (number 54)	Cell.M.
ASHFORD	9.2.16		Nil	Cell.M.
ASHFORD	10.2.16		Nil	Cell.M.
ASHFORD	11.2.16		Nil	Cell.M.
ASHFORD	12.2.16		Nil	Cell.M.
ASHFORD	13.2.16		Nil	Cell.M.
ASHFORD	14.2.16		Nil	Cell.M.

Army Form C. 2118

WAR DIARY
or
INTELLIGENCE SUMMARY
(Erase heading not required.)

Instructions regarding War Diaries and Intelligence Summaries are contained in F. S. Regs., Part II. and the Staff Manual respectively. Title Pages will be prepared in manuscript.

Place	Date	Hour	Summary of Events and Information	Remarks and references to Appendices
ASHFORD	15.2.16		nil	
ASHFORD	16.2.16		nil	
ASHFORD	17.2.16		nil	
ASHFORD	18.2.16		nil	
ASHFORD	19.2.16		nil	
ASHFORD	20.2.16		nil	
ASHFORD	21.2.16		nil	
ASHFORD	22.2.16		nil	
ASHFORD	23.2.16		nil	
ASHFORD	24.2.16	6 p.m.	"State of Readiness" commenced.	
ASHFORD	25.2.16		nil	
ASHFORD	26.2.16	6 p.m.	5 Officers joined the Battalion from 3rd line at BLACKPOOL in excess of Establishment	
ASHFORD	27.2.16		nil	
ASHFORD	28.2.16		nil	
ASHFORD	29.2.16		nil	

J. G. Grey Heim
Lieut. Colonel,
Comdg. 4/5 Loyal North Lancs Regt.